THE TREASURES OF ST PETERSBURG AND THE
HERMITAGE

This publication accompanies a three-part TV series exploring the treasures of St Petersburg and the Hermitage for Five Television. It is a selective celebration of one of the most extraordinary achievements of human creativity over the past 300 years and is intended to convey something of the pleasure of a visit to the city and its great museum.

By Graham Addicott

St

Petersburg is, quite simply, the glory of Russia – perhaps the only world-class city created almost as a work of art in itself. Founded by Peter the Great in 1703 and celebrating its 300th birthday on 27 May 2003, it was for 200 years the imperial capital of the tsars, including Catherine the Great and Nicholas II. It has been the home of writers such as Pushkin and Dostoyevsky, of Pavlova and the Bolshoi Ballet, of composers Tchaikovsky and Shostakovich.

The birthplace of Vladimir Putin, the current president of Russia, saw the start of the Bolshevik Revolution and Lenin's return to Russia to take the reins of power, and was the site of one of the most legendary sieges of the Second World War. Its name has been changed from St Petersburg to Petrograd, to Leningrad and now back to St Petersburg as the city has remained at the centre of the continual struggle of the Russian people to define themselves. And at its heart sits what is – despite rivalry from the Louvre in Paris, the Metropolitan in New York and the British Museum in London – probably the greatest museum in the world, the State Hermitage.

The institution began life as the Winter Palace, a home of emperors and empresses before becoming a showcase for their treasures. Both its exterior and much of the interior attest to their wealth and power. The museum has survived

The façade of the Winter Palace
Facing page: a home and showcase for emperors and empresses and now the centrepiece of the Hermitage museum complex

Grigory Semyonovich Musikiysky Portrait of Peter I, 1723
This small enamel painting on gold shows the emperor and founder of the city of St Petersburg with the Peter and Paul Fortress and Trinity Square visible in the background

Christian Gottlob Hammer View of St Petersburg, c.1840
The image of a thriving city shows a panorama across the River Neva with St Isaac's Cathedral, the Admiralty and the Winter Palace dominating the scene

Stalin's rule of terror and the 900-day siege of Leningrad, and is now facing another challenge – to adapt to conditions in a twenty-first-century capitalist Russia.

Love, murder and politics have all had an effect on the Hermitage's collections. As a result of being nationalised after the Revolution of 1917 its holdings expanded to fill not just the palace, but the three pavilions built on to it in the late eighteenth century. Large numbers of paintings and other works of art were "acquired" from the defeated ruling class by the Soviet state, such as the fabulous Shchukin and Morozov collections of modern masters including Van Gogh, Gauguin and Matisse. The Hermitage collection is now huge – more than three million items, including more than 12,000 sculptures, 16,000 paintings, 600,000 drawings and prints and 266,000 works of applied art, to say nothing of a million coins and medals. It's an often-quoted "factoid" that even if you were just to glance at each one, it would take nine years to view the lot. Perhaps luckily for visitors, only a tiny percentage is ever on show at any one time.

The Winter Palace remains the centrepiece of the museum complex, which incorporates the Hermitage Theatre, the Small Hermitage, the New Hermitage and the Old Hermitage, and is a work of blue, white and gold over-the-top Baroque by Italian architect Bartolomeo Rastrelli, built on the banks of the river Neva between 1754 and 1762. About 400 three-quarter columns in two tiers create the visual effect of tremendous height, assisted by window cornices getting bigger from the ground to the third floor, and by 90 statues and 40 decorative vases along the roof parapet. It is as much a work of art as anything contained within it.

The Hermitage today, seen along the Dvortsovaya (or Palace) Embankment
On the right is the Winter Palace, built by Bartolomeo Rastrelli for the Empress Elizabeth, completed in 1762. In the middle is the Small Hermitage, built by Vallin de la Mothe for Catherine the Great, completed in 1770 and the Old Hermitage, built by Yury Velten, completed in 1787. Finally, on the far left, is the New Hermitage, built by Leo von Klenze for Nicholas I, completed in 1852. This eclectic but sympathetic mixture of classical architecture was thus created by Italian, French, German and Russian architects. Below: the ground floor plan of the Hermitage

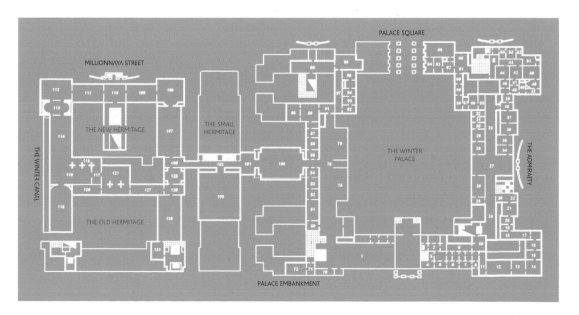

The Jordan Staircase
Also known as the Ambassadors'
Staircase, the lavish main entrance
to Rastrelli's Winter Palace was
built between 1754 and 1762 and
painted by Konstantin Andreevich
Ukhtomsky after restoration
following the fire of 1837

The Pavilion Hall
This room in the Small Hermitage
was re-modelled by Leo von Klenze
in Moorish style for Nicholas I

Grigory Semyonovich Musikiysky
Portrait of Catherine I with a View
of Yekaterinhof, 1724
The wife of Peter I is shown in
this enamel work on gold with
the palace he built for her in the
background. She wears the star and
sash of the Order of St Catherine

The Kolyvan Vase
A huge jasper boulder was found
on the slopes of Revnevaya in the
Altai Mountains. For two years the
stone was hand-chiselled on the
spot and then taken to the nearby
Kolyvan lapidary works by 500
labourers using rollers, ropes and
horses. Following a design by
Russian architect Avraam Melnikov,
the vase was crafted at the factory
from 1831 to 1843. It then took
nine months, using 160 horses,
to drag it (dismantled) to the
Hermitage. It weighs nineteen
tons and, with the base, is more
than 2.5 metres tall

IMPERIAL SPLENDOURS OF CATHERINE II

History has treated Catherine the Great cruelly. She is perhaps popularly best known for her alleged sexual appetites rather than for her appreciation of the arts and architecture. Yet if any one person is responsible for the Hermitage, and much else in St Petersburg today, it is the empress. In her time she purchased more than 4,000 Old Master paintings, which form the core of the museum's collections. But her interests – and acquisitions – went much wider. Although not particularly enamoured of sculpture, she bought the only Michelangelo marble in the museum, the unfinished *Crouching Boy*, and commissioned Jean-Antoine Houdon's *Voltaire* (1778), a life-size piece depicting the philosopher (with whom Catherine used to correspond) in old age. It's also because of her that the Hermitage has the best collection of French eighteenth-century bronzes outside France.

Catherine shopped until she dropped and most historians now agree that her spree really started with her purchase of Dutch Old Master paintings from the Berlin dealer, Johann Gotzkowski, in 1764. According to the art historian and deputy director of the Menshikov Palace, Galina Rodionova, there were three major reasons why the empress was attracted to Dutch paintings: the Dutch were willing to sell; the works were relatively inexpensive; and the Dutch style was at the time modern, even revolutionary. One of her first acquisitions was Jan Steen's *The Revellers*, a classic of the genre. Famous for his tavern scenes with a keen sense of humour and an affection for even the most mundane objects – a left-behind slipper, a broken clay pipe –

Michelangelo Buonarroti
Crouching Boy, c.1530-1534
Catherine the Great was not much interested in sculpture, but she still managed to acquire this beautiful marble piece, the only work by Michelangelo in the Hermitage collection. The sculpture is widely believed to have been made by the High Renaissance maestro for the Medici Chapel in the church of San Lorenzo in Florence, where it was intended as a figure in mourning to be placed on the upper platform of one of the vast family tombs

Jean-Antoine Houdon
Voltaire, 1781
Catherine II commissioned this statue in 1780. She greatly admired Voltaire and had corresponded with him from 1763 until his death in 1778. She even bought his library and manuscripts from the niece who had inherited them. This is the most vivid and polished of all Houdon's sculptural portraits of the famed writer and philosopher. Voltaire posed for the master not long before his death and is here portrayed as a frail old man, yet the sculptor managed to convey the inner fire that burned within him

Jan Steen
The Revellers, c.1660
This painting, called by the Hermitage *The Revellers*, but also known as *The Idlers*, is one of Steen's masterpieces. The amusing and lively characters are the artist himself and his wife Margaret, daughter of the landscape painter Jan van Goyen

he was among the first of the Western European painters to depict "real life" in an age when most works were more studied. Another was *Portrait of a Young Man with a Glove* (c.1650), by Frans Hals, whose use of rough brush strokes led him to be dubbed "the Impressionist of Dutch painting". She also bought *Breakfast with a Crab* (1648), by Willem Claesz Heda, probably his best still-life. Objects in his paintings were almost devoid of bright colours. But, says Galina Rodionova, they all reveal a hidden beauty and the lemon against the white tablecloth "feels bitter in your mouth".

Engraved gems were one of the empress's main loves and she collected Greek and Roman examples, as well as Renaissance pieces. She also bought Classical sculpture and set the scene for Russia's great archaeological discoveries by annexing the Crimea in 1783. In the applied arts, she commissioned silver, jewels, porcelain, tapestries and other works from the leading craftsmen of the day. The Wedgwood Green Frog dinner service is a prime example. The empress also had a passion for all things British (see page 27), not just acquiring collections, but encouraging artists who were undervalued in their homeland and are now regarded as among the finest painters of their time, such as Joseph Wright of Derby. She paid British architects and gardeners to come to the imperial capital and help to create "a little bit of England".

Catherine was absolutely driven by the ⟫⟶

Tiziano Vecellio, known as Titian
The Repentant Mary Magdalene,
c.1560
This picture is claimed by many to be Titian's masterpiece. Certainly it was produced at a time when the artist was at the height of his powers, and the style of painting is more sophisticated than in his earlier works, more saturated with shades. The colours are extremely close to one another, creating an almost monochromatic result

Willem Claesz Heda
Breakfast with a Crab, 1648
The outstanding accomplishments of Dutch still-life painters are represented in the Hermitage by the works of the masters of the genre – Pieter Claesz, Willem Kalf and Willem Claesz Heda. This painting by Heda is probably his best still-life. It is almost devoid of bright colours and thus, according to art historian Galina Rodionova, "you can taste the lemon"

Frans Hals
Portrait of a Young Man with a Glove, c.1650
This is one of two works in the Hermitage collection by the greatest portrait painter of the seventeenth century. Most of his peers approached their pictures slowly, with preparatory drawings, a certain amount of under-painting and an elaborate finish. Although there is no conclusive evidence of his method, Hals seems to have started directly on the canvas and painted quickly, leaving his first spontaneous expression – almost an oil sketch – as the finished work. He continued to use this technique, which gave a striking immediacy to his portrayals of character, all his life, painting with increasing freedom as he grew older

**Michelangelo Merisi da Caravaggio
The Lute Player, c.1595**
Caravaggio's seemingly
straightforward painting contains,
as did many works of the period,
an allegorical message – that
youth and beauty are fleeting.
This is conveyed by the broken
string of the bow and a crack on
the tabletop. Also, the flowers
are fresh, but cut, so will soon
die, while music itself is transient

Peter Paul Rubens
Bacchus, c.1638-1640
This late work by the Flemish master shows a grotesque image of the Roman god of wine surrounded by nymphs and satyrs, who indulge in their passion for drink. Often such images were celebratory, but here there is a sense of excess to the point of corpulence and self-destruction

Rembrandt Harmenszoon van Rijn
Flora, 1634
Although named after the goddess of spring and flowers, this painting is actually a portrait of the artist's wife Saskia, and is as well known by that name as it is by its title of *Flora*. Rembrandt painted Saskia as the goddess three times. She died in 1642, shortly after giving birth to their fourth child

Rembrandt's acid attack

One of the stranger social developments of the late twentieth century was the way in which works of art became a target of protest. And one of the most shocking examples of this occurred at the Hermitage in 1985 when a Lithuanian threw acid at Rembrandt's *Danaë* and stabbed it twice. In the immediate aftermath, a strong jet of water to clean off the acid would have affected the painting, so staff gulped mouthfuls of water out of bowls and sprayed it gently across the surface.

However, the damage was still substantial – as the acid had rolled down the canvas it picked up varnish, and the varnish in turn picked up paint. There was pressure from the government to restore the work as quickly as possible. But the museum restorers resisted and, according to Catherine Phillips of the Hermitage Development Trust, said they wanted to conserve it damaged as it was, rather than re-paint Rembrandt: "They left it so long that in the end they were able to restore it as much as they felt

necessary, or proper – which was to leave what was Rembrandt; to fill in just slightly where there had been serious acid damage."

It took twelve years to complete the restoration, but now the painting – first brought to Russia by Catherine the Great – is back on display. Much of the detail (of the story of the seduction of the king of Argos's daughter by Jupiter, who disguised himself as a shower of gold) has disappeared, leaving areas of under-paint open to view. But Rembrandt's genius shines through.

desire to develop a national culture that was an extension the French model which the founder of St Petersburg, Peter the Great, had instituted. She was a committed follower of the Enlightenment and, in leaps and bounds, she westernised Russia. Her acquisitions were always made by combining this aspiration for her country with her personal tastes.

One of her great coups was the purchase of 500 paintings owned by Pierre Crozat, a French banker who had amassed the most important private collection formed in France in the early eighteenth century. These reached the Hermitage in 1722 and among them were nine Rembrandts, not least the *Danaë* (1636), which has become virtually the symbol of the museum (see page 16), six works by Van Dyck, including a *Self-Portrait* (c.1630), some outstanding Rubens oil sketches, Raphael's *Holy Family* (1502-1503), Giorgione's *Judith* (late 1500s) and Veronese's *Lamentation over the Dead Christ* (1576-1582).

Perhaps her "best buy", at the very least in terms of kudos, was her acquisition of the Walpole Collection (see page 31), but it wasn't her only famous British purchase. In 1773 Catherine ordered the Green Frog service from Josiah Wedgwood's factory in Staffordshire – the largest and most important dinner service that it had ever produced. Each piece is decorated with a different view – 1,222 in all – faithfully recording castles, abbeys,

Josiah Wedgwood
The Green Frog service, 1773-1774
This creamware service, in a style typical of items produced by Wedgwood, was commissioned by Catherine the Great in 1773. It was intended for the Chesme Palace – at one time called La Grenouillere or Kekerekeksinen because of its location on a frog marsh, hence the green frog emblem on every one of the 952 pieces. The historical value of the 1,222 views of buildings and landscapes in various parts of Britain, together with the variety of forms and refined combination of colours, make it a star of the Hermitage's English ceramics collection

stately homes, gardens, towns and landscapes throughout Britain. It is a snapshot of the country at the time. A green frog was added to each since the service (for 50 place settings) was intended for the Kekerekeksinen, or "frog marsh", Palace (later known as the Chesme Palace).

Not everything was so practical. One of the most impressive rooms in the Hermitage, the Raphael Loggia, is, legend has it, a result of the empress having a "bad hair day". On 1 September 1778 it was raining. Cold and bored, Catherine was leafing through the drawings of frescoes by Raphael and there and then decided to have her own Raphael Loggia in Russia. She ordered architect Giacomo Quarenghi, who had built the Hermitage Theatre for her, to design a magnificently long and high gallery, lit by windows looking out over the Winter Canal, and dispatched Russian artists to Rome to make copies of the frescoes of Raphael's gallery in the Vatican Palace. Every surface, wall and vault is covered with the paintings.

Gradually, architecture took over from other art forms as Catherine's main obsession. Many of St Petersburg's greatest architectural masterpieces, including the Winter Palace, the Smolny Cathedral and the Tauride Palace, were completed during her reign. She eventually shrugged off the Baroque as vulgar and Rastrelli, who had created the Catherine Palace at Tsarskoe Selo in just that style, had to retire. A purer Neo-Classicism, marked by its imitation of antiquity, was now her style of choice. Vallin de la Mothe designed the New Hermitage for her and Scotsman Charles Cameron became "Architect to Her Imperial Highness" (see page 23).

The Raphael Loggia
Created by Giacomo Quarenghi between 1778 and 1785 for Catherine the Great, this is a replica of Raphael's celebrated gallery in the Vatican in Rome

Smolny Cathedral, 1748-1757
Rastrelli's inspired combination of European Baroque and old Russian style produced a building like no other in the world

The Green Dining Room and the Bedchamber of Maria Federovna
Below and bottom: these rooms in the Catherine Palace were both designed by the Scottish architect Charles Cameron in the 1780s

Tsarskoe Selo

The emperors and empresses of Russia built a number of glorious palaces on the outskirts of St Petersburg. But none is more evocative of the heyday and twilight years of the Romanovs than the Catherine Palace and the Alexander Palace at Tsarskoe Selo. The former was a favourite of Catherine the Great, while the latter was where Nicholas II and his family lived and were held under house arrest before being taken to Yekaterinburg to be murdered.

It is undoubtedly the Catherine Palace and its sprawling parks that impress the most. In its present form it owes its existence to Empress Elizabeth (1709-1761) who, having had a palace built there using three different architects, decided to scrap the project and get her new Italian architect, Bartolomeo Rastrelli, to create a vast Baroque masterpiece. Elizabeth and Rastrelli were made for each other in their love of theatrical excess and she was so pleased with the result that she named it after her mother, Catherine I. The long façade, 1,000ft of turquoise and gold, features 60 monumental figures of Atlas supporting the upper storeys on their bent and straining necks. Inside, there is a seemingly endless sequence of rooms, their walls lined with agate, jasper, malachite and other precious and semi-precious materials. The most spectacular is the Great Ballroom, where Elizabeth hosted her famous costume balls, dressing herself as either a Dutch sailor or a Chevalier guard.

Catherine the Great used to

receive foreign dignitaries here in the huge gold and mirrored hall, but, in the opinion of Colin Amery, director of World Monuments Fund Britain, Rastrelli's great achievement is what is called the Gold Suite – a gilded procession of rooms for the court, at the end of which lies the ballroom: "You would be completely gob-smacked by the time you arrived in the ballroom; you would be exhausted with the splendour – and that's how you were meant to feel." Privately, though, Catherine II's tastes rose to higher things. Thus, the Cameron Gallery and the Agate Rooms.

The Alexander Palace is a much more sombre affair. It is regarded by some as architect Giacomo Quarenghi's masterpiece, with its lemon-yellow façade spanned by a gigantic colonnade. Many of the last tsar's family possessions are still on show in one of the wings, including toys and the uniforms once worn by the doomed children. Perhaps because history here is relatively recent, the exhibition is surprisingly heart-wrenching.

The Catherine Palace
The seemingly endless grandeur of Rastrelli's designs add up to perhaps the greatest Baroque vision in all of Russia. Left: the main façade. Top: the Great Hall. Above: the Picture Gallery. All were built between 1752 and 1756

21

The émigré architect

Cameron's creations
Facing page: the Great Hall of the Agate Pavilion. Above and left: the Cameron Gallery. Below: the park at Pavlovsk, with buildings and landscape designed by Charles Cameron between 1781 and 1786 on the orders of Catherine the Great for her son, the future Paul I

Charles Cameron (1743-1811) is the mystery man of architecture. Scottish born, but virtually unknown in his homeland, or in the West for that matter, he is responsible for some of the finest architectural works of the eighteenth century. Perhaps the most outstanding of these is the Cameron Gallery at Tsarskoe Selo, Russia's Versailles just outside St Petersburg.

Commissioned by Catherine the Great, it is, according to South Bank University architectural lecturer Paul Davies, "slender; lean and mean" – a perfect Neo-Classical foil to the Baroque Catherine Palace created by architect Bartolomeo Rastrelli. This was not to say that Cameron disliked Rastrelli's style. In fact, it is claimed that on his way to work each morning he doffed his hat to the Italian's creation and was continually adapting and amending his design to harmonise with it. Described by Pushkin as a "huge hall soaring towards the clouds", the Cameron Gallery dominates the Catherine Gardens at Tsarskoe Selo. With its glass-covered pavilion it allowed the empress to stroll out of the main palace whatever the

weather to admire the view across the "Great Pond". The staircase up to it is striking because of its oval shape, giving the impression that the gallery is hovering above the ground. Among the antique statues installed beneath the open arcades was a bust of Charles James Fox, arch enemy of British prime minister William Pitt the Younger, whom Catherine could not stand.

Another of Cameron's gems is the fabulous Agate Rooms, also at Tsarskoe Selo, which flaunt all the mineral wealth of the Russian Empire, including (not surprisingly) agate as well as jasper, malachite and lapis lazuli. Catherine often held intimate dinner parties here and the main room has a magnificent parquet floor – one of the few features of Tsarskoe Selo to have survived in its original state through the palace's occupation by the Nazis during the siege of what was then Leningrad.

Cameron was born to the wealthy family of a master builder and in 1767 moved to Rome, where he studied and surveyed ancient monuments, in particular the baths. On returning to England he published a book on baths entitled

Roman Thermae in 1772. This so impressed Catherine that she summoned him to St Petersburg and made him "Architect to Her Imperial Highness" – despite the fact that at that stage he had built nothing. Combining the empress's tastes and habits with his imagination, he was responsible for some of the most dazzling and original large-scale architectural creations of the eighteenth

century, as well as for bringing out a horde of British architects, craftsmen and gardeners to help to transform towns, villages and buildings throughout the country.

Cameron spent more than 30 years in Russia, and died there, without ever bothering to learn the language. Despite this, the Russians with whom he lived and worked honoured him by calling him "Karl Karlovich".

The Amber Room at Tsarskoe Selo

"The Amber Room is almost more famous for not being there" – Colin Amery, director, World Monuments Fund Britain.

Created by German craftsmen for the Prussian king's palace near Berlin, the unfinished Amber Room was given to the visiting Peter the Great in 1716 by the king's son and heir, Frederick William I. Russian craftsmen, under German supervision, eventually completed it and installed it in the Catherine Palace in the mid-eighteenth century. It was the largest work of art ever made out of amber, weighing some six tons, and, for extra radiance, was backed entirely in gold leaf.

Not a whole room *per se*, it comprised a series of large wall panels covering an area a little more than ten square yards inlaid with several tons of masterfully carved high-quality amber, long mirrors and four Florentine mosaics made of semi-precious stones such as quartz, jasmine, jade and onyx, which depicted allegorical scenes of the five senses.

In 1941, as the Germans advanced on Stalingrad, the Russians attempted to hide the work by wallpapering over it, but a Nazi "art protection officer", boasting a degree in art history, took one look and ordered it to be transported to German territory for "safety". It took six men 36 hours to dismantle and pack it into 28 crates for the journey to Königsberg Castle (in what is now Kaliningrad) in East Prussia on the Baltic coast. The town stands on large deposits of amber and was meant to be its original home.

At the end of the war the Russians razed the castle to the ground and the Amber Room went missing. Did it melt during RAF bombing raids? Did it escape on board the German liner, the *Wilhelm Gustloff*, only to be torpedoed by a Russian submarine? Or is it still buried under Weimar County Hall? Nobody knows, although many have claimed otherwise. In 1991, for example, while on a visit to Germany, President Yeltsin said he had proof that it was hidden in a former Nazi bunker, but when the authorities looked, they found nothing.

People have spent years searching for the Amber Room, valued at today's prices at more than £70 million, and one mosaic surfaced in Germany in 1997. By 1979, however, the Soviet Union had abandoned any effort to recover the original, deciding instead to rebuild it based on old photographs and the reminiscences of past museum curators. Work finally began in 1982 after various obstacles were overcome, the most important of which was the rediscovery of the forgotten skills of ancient amber guilds. Old methods of cutting and carving had to be re-learned, but most challenging was unlocking the eighteenth-century mystery of dyeing amber, a process essential to enhancing the stunning effect of the Amber Room. Credit for that achievement goes to the Mendeleyev Chemical Institute in St Petersburg, and the new-found knowledge is now a closely guarded secret.

The Russians had been able to whisk most of the 100 or so objects in the original collection to safety in Siberia. These included tables, jewellery boxes and chess sets made of amber, many of which have been installed in the newly reconstructed Amber Room.

Amber visions then and now
Below: hand-tinted photograph of the original room, c.1930. Below right: close-up detail of carving from the reconstructed Amber Room. Right and facing page: the reconstruction of the Amber Room, 1982-2003

The peacock and the duchess

Every Wednesday at 5pm people gather in the Pavilion Hall of the Winter Palace for the chiming of the Peacock Clock. As the bells start to play an owl moves his head from side to side. The peacock, which stands on a metal hillock, begins to spread his tail while at the same time nodding his head. He then executes a 180-degree turn to display his tail feathers from behind. Finally, a metal cockerel lifts his head and starts to crow. The clock face is on the head of a mushroom under a gilt-bronze oak tree and a dragonfly sitting on the mushroom marks the seconds.

The timepiece was made in 1772 by the London jeweller, James Cox, best known for the jewel-encrusted clocks he produced for the Oriental market. But if the clock is extraordinary, so is its history. It was commissioned by the Duchess of Kingston, who arrived in St Petersburg in 1777, having left England after being found guilty of bigamy. In 1744 she had secretly married a young naval lieutenant, Augustus Hervey, who later became the third Earl of Bristol; then in 1769 she went on to marry the fabulously wealthy Duke of Kingston, who died four years later. The duchess, renowned in London society for her many escapades – including attending the Venetian ambassador's ball naked – only escaped the death penalty by exercising her rights as a peer of the realm.

Having paid her fine, she had a ship built which was big enough to take her and all her possessions to the northern capital of Russia in some style. Catherine the Great, no stranger to scandal herself, immediately took to the duchess and gave her a beautiful house in St Petersburg. When she died in Paris in 1788 she left an elaborate will that was fought over by a number of claimants. The Peacock Clock ended up in the possession of Grigory Potemkin, Catherine's lover, who gave it to his empress.

The duchess had brought the clock to St Petersburg carefully disassembled, with hundreds of pieces of mechanism packed separately. It took a mechanic two years, from 1792 to 1794, to make it work. Even today it has its own minder, known as the "Head of The Hermitage Clock Lab", whose function is to service it, as well as oversee the Wednesday chimings.

**Thomas Gainsborough
Portrait of a Lady, c.1770**
This painting is said to be of Elizabeth Chudleigh, the bigamous Duchess of Kingston who commissioned the Peacock Clock (above)

THE BRITISH CONNECTION

"Catherine the Great had a passion for all things British. She was very badly struck with Anglomania. If you really want to see certain aspects of British eighteenth-century art, you have to go to Russia to see them; you cannot see them here [in the UK]"
Timothy Stevens, director, the Hermitage Rooms at Somerset House.

British influences are everywhere in St Petersburg, as are those of the Italians and the French. For St Petersburg is, above all, a meeting of Europe and Russia, or perhaps, more accurately, a European metropolis created on Russian soil. The cityscape, with its canals, Baroque and Rococo buildings and the Neva running through its heart, is more reminiscent of Amsterdam, London and Rome than it is of Moscow or Vladivostock. It was Peter the Great who set the ball rolling in 1703 with his desire to drag the country from what he saw as its "backward" Muscovy past into a Western world of progress and enlightenment. In the words of author Orlando Figes: "St Petersburg was more than a city. It was a vast, almost utopian, project of cultural engineering to reconstruct the Russian

as a European man." But it was his heirs and successors – particularly Catherine the Great – who had the most effect on how the city looks and the artistic treasures it contains today.

Enter the British. Catherine brought in hordes of British landscape designers and architects to help to create her vision. Among them was Charles Cameron (see page 23), whose creations included the Cameron Gallery and the Agate Rooms. James Cox's Peacock mechanical clock plays to rapturous acclaim in the Pavilion Room of the Winter Palace to this day (see page 26). The Hermitage also has outstanding examples of English silver, not least the famous Jerningham wine-cooler by Charles Kandler, a copy of which was made by, and is on display in, London's Victoria and Albert Museum. Some of the best works of Josiah Wedgwood, including pieces from the celebrated Green Frog service, decorate cases in the imperial apartments. The museum has an extremely rare collection of engraved gems from Britain, and there are precious snuff boxes, pocket watches and clocks made by British craftsmen who in some cases lived and worked in St Petersburg.

The collection of British paintings in the ⤚⤚→

Jerningham wine-cooler
This remarkable piece was made by Charles Kandler in London from 1734 to 1735

**Joseph Wright of Derby
The Iron Forge Viewed from
Without, 1773**
This was the last of five pictures on
the theme of the iron forge painted
by Joseph Wright between 1771
and 1773. It was the first of three
works by the English painter to be
acquired by the Hermitage and has
remained a favoured work in the
collection. In the early part of the
twentieth century the illustrious
Russian critic and artist Alexandre
Benois was moved to write: "This
picture serves as a marvellous
piece of evidence of Wright's
technical perfection. To this day
it enraptures with the grace of its
contrasts, the depth of the dark
areas and the soft force of the
lighting... Wright's picture presents
us with a piece of life just as it
was presented directly to its
author, and this is perhaps its
greatest virtue."

Hermitage is not of great size compared with the Dutch, French or Italian departments, but it contains, for instance, masterpieces by Joseph Wright of Derby, including his superb *Iron Forge* (1773) and *Firework Display at the Castel Sant Angelo in Rome (La Girandola)* (1774-1775). For Catherine II, Joshua Reynolds painted his *Infant Hercules Strangling the Serpents* (1786-1788), a symbol for the empress of the young Russia gaining strength and emerging on to the world stage. And Richard Brompton produced one of the most well-known portraits of Catherine herself. The museum also has several canvases by Angelica Kauffmann, one of the first two women to be honoured by the Royal Academy, and enough pieces by Scottish painter Christina Robertson to mount a travelling exhibition shown in Edinburgh in the mid-1990s. Thomas Gainsborough's *A Woman in Blue* (c.1780) entered the museum in 1912 from the collection of the master of the hunt at the imperial court, Aleksei Z Khitrovo.

One of the best British collections acquired by the Hermitage was the Walpole Collection, amassed by Sir Robert Walpole, Britain's first prime minister, for his gallery at Houghton Hall in Norfolk. Snapped up by Catherine the Great from his grandson at a bargain price, it included twenty Van Dycks, nineteen Rubens, eight Titians, five Murillos, three works each by Veronese and Guido Reni, two by Velázquez, a Frans Hals, a Raphael and a Poussin. At the time this caused an enormous scandal as the collection had been destined to form the foundation of a national gallery in England. The purchase may well have been motivated as much by politics as passion for art. Britain was then at the zenith of its power with an empire "on which the sun never sets". Catherine was, some historians claim, demonstrating that the Russian Empire could upstage the British.

The Hermitage, too, seems to have learned the art of empire-style expansion, as, since 2000, it has been opening "mini-Hermitages" overseas. It is fitting perhaps that the first was the Hermitage Rooms at London's Somerset House. In this miniature version of the Winter Palace rotating themed exhibitions of treasures from the St Petersburg parent are held, while computer terminals offer virtual tours of the real thing.

**Thomas Gainsborough
Portrait of a Lady in Blue, c.1780**
This is probably the best British painting in the Hermitage, which only acquired it in 1912 from the collection of Aleksei Z Khitrovo, the master of the hunt at the imperial court. It was initially listed as a portrait of the Duchess of Beaufort, but there is no evidence to support this. Instead, the silvery-blue image is enhanced by a certain mystery surrounding the beautiful sitter. "If ever the nation should produce genius sufficient to acquire to us the honourable distinction of an English school," wrote Sir Joshua Reynolds, "the name of Gainsborough will be transmitted to posterity in the history of art, among the very first of that rising fame."

**Joshua Reynolds
The Infant Hercules Strangling the Serpents, 1788**
This classically inspired painting in Reynolds's aspiring Grand Manner style was commissioned from the artist directly by Catherine the Great. It is an allegorical work using the story of the infant Hercules as a symbol of Russia's growing strength

NEW IMPRESSIONS

It is a curious trick of fate that Moscow, symbol of old Russia to many from St Petersburg, should have supplied the Hermitage with the paintings for which it is possibly best known outside Russia – the magnificent Impressionist and Post-Impressionist works from the collections of Sergei Shchukin and Ivan Morozov. The two men were merchants and their collections, formed at the turn of the nineteenth and twentieth centuries, were seized by the state following the 1917 Revolution. After a lifetime of collecting and commissioning (see page 34) Shchukin owned thirteen Monets, 37 Matisses, sixteen Gauguins, five works by Degas, sixteen Derains, nine Marquets, four Van Goghs, eight Cézannes and 50 Picassos. Morozov had more than 400 works by Russian painters – most of which are now in the Tretiakov Gallery, Moscow – including some by a then little known artist, Marc Chagall. He also acquired pictures by Spanish painters Joaquin Sorolla and Ignacio Zuloaga, Sisley and Pissarro landscapes and Renoir's *Portrait of the Actress Jeanne Samary* (1878). In 1907 he embarked on a huge buying spree, adding Gauguin and Cézanne to the collection.

Following their post-Revolution nationalisation the collections made up the holdings of the Museum of Contemporary Western Art in Moscow. When it closed in 1948, they were divided between the Pushkin Museum in Moscow and the Hermitage, the latter receiving more than 200 pictures. At first, because of the prevailing political climate (Soviet art policy deemed them degenerate), only the most conservative, realist paintings could be shown – an Albert Marquet view, for instance, and *Rouen Cathedral* (1908) by Emile-Othon Friesz. After Stalin's death things got a little better.

In 1956, the museum mounted a major exhibition of French paintings down the ages and showed almost everything – though not the Cubist Picassos. Matisse's *Music* (1910) and *The Dance II* (1910) were hung on the stairs where it was hoped they would escape serious scrutiny by the authorities. The pictures stayed on display after the show closed and gradually others were added. A new guided tour of French art was devised, beginning with Neo-Classicism and running up to Picasso. But in 1963 the whole ⟫→

Pierre Auguste Renoir
Portrait of the Actress Jeanne Samary, 1878
"What a marvellous girl," said the artist, recalling the Comédie Française actress whose portrait is one of the most striking attractions of the Impressionist collections at the Hermitage. "And what a skin! She was positively radiating light."

Paul Cézanne
The Smoker, c.1895
The Hermitage has eleven works by Cézanne. As an artist he declared he wanted "to make of Impressionism something solid and durable, like the art of the museums". When portraying people Cézanne never tried to convey their psychological state or character. Humans were for him primarily the most complex and interesting form created by nature

Music and The Dance II

Henri Matisse (1869-1954) is acknowledged as one of the greatest artists of the twentieth century, and the Hermitage contains some of the finest examples of his work.

Two paintings of the "once seen, never forgotten" variety are *Music* (below right) and *The Dance II*. (The first version of *The Dance* is now in the Museum of Modern Art in New York. In effect it is a full-sized sketch from 1909. The Hermitage picture is the finished work whose vivid colour makes it perhaps the most dynamic image of dance ever painted.) Their history is as fascinating as the paintings.

Both were commissioned from the artist in the spring of 1909 by merchant and industrialist Sergei Shchukin to decorate the staircase of the Trubetskoy Palace, his Moscow home. He already knew Matisse's *Joie de Vivre* (1906), which belonged to his American friends and fellow patrons, Leo and Gertrude Stein. In the background of the painting can be glimpsed a tiny ring of dancers – the inspiration for *The Dance II* (right).

Once he'd commissioned the works, Shchukin started to get cold feet. He wrote to Matisse: "I have taken three young girls (eight, nine and ten years old) into the house – and here in Russia (we are somewhat Oriental here) one cannot show nudes to young girls. Make the same circle but with girls in dresses." The artist refused and sent the completed panel of *The Dance II*. Shchukin wrote back: "I find your panel of such nobility that I have decided to defy our bourgeois opinion and to place on my staircase a subject with nudes."

In fact, before shipping the two panels to Moscow, Matisse had exhibited them at the Salon d'Automne and had been subjected to a torrent of abuse. One newspaper cartoon depicted a horrified mother whisking her children out of the exhibition. Shchukin had been in Paris and seen the fuss the show created – his resolve buckled and he bought another painting for his staircase.

On the train back to Moscow the merchant was overcome by his own "weakness and lack of courage", writing to Matisse: "One should not quit the field of battle without attempting combat. For this reason I have decided to exhibit your panels. People will make a clamour and laugh, but since I am convinced that you are on the right path, time will perhaps be on my side." But his courage failed him again and, worried about how the artist had graphically (for the time) portrayed the flautist's genitalia in *Music*, he actually painted them out himself.

When Matisse announced he was coming to Moscow in 1911, Shchukin was petrified at the prospect of the painter seeing what had been done to his work. In the event, it seems the artist stood in silence in front of the "censored" paintings for some time and then said: "It doesn't change anything."

The painting remained in that state until 1988, when a Hermitage curator (the panels were now part of the museum's collection) asked the restoration department if the over-painting could be removed. It turned out that Shchukin, by accident or deliberately, had used a water-soluble solution to cover the offending parts, and it was cleaned off with a sponge.

Shchukin had been right when he asserted that time may have been on his side: the panels are now regarded as among the best works of Post-Impressionism in Russia.

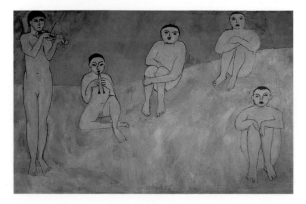

Claude Oscar Monet
Lady in the Garden (Sainte-Adresse), 1867
There are eight paintings in the Hermitage by the man responsible for the word "Impressionism" (from his painting *Impression, Sunrise*). Originally used in a derogatory sense, it came to be the generally accepted term to describe a whole art movement. The museum's collection spans Monet's career, from early works such as *Lady in the Garden (Sainte-Adresse)* to *Waterloo Bridge*, painted at the beginning of the twentieth century

Vincent van Gogh
Lilac Bush, 1889
Lilac Bush was painted in May of 1889 in the garden of the asylum at St Rémy, near Arles, just a year before Van Gogh committed suicide. The tragic undertone can be seen in the colour scheme of the canvas – in the violent clash of its saturated blues and greens

Pierre Auguste Renoir
Girl with a Fan, 1881
There are six Renoirs in the Hermitage and all of them demonstrate the best qualities of this Impressionist. The "beautiful Alphoncine", daughter of the owner of a famous French tavern of the time, turns under the painter's brush into the somewhat mysterious *Girl With a Fan*

praesidium of the Moscow Academy of Art descended on the Hermitage intending to stop the display of the Shchukin-Morozov Impressionists and Post-Impressionists as its members felt they were having a corrupting effect on young Russian artists. After viewing the paintings, the men from Moscow started to argue that they should be removed, at which point one of the museum's senior staff requested permission to read from the decree which had nationalised the Shchukin collection in the first place. It described it as being "of high national significance in the matter of public education". "Who wrote that nonsense?" screamed the head of the Moscow delegation. "It is signed Ulyanov Lenin," replied the Hermitage staff member. It was a short-lived victory, however: within two years the apparatchiks had removed most of the pictures from public display.

Nowadays, Monet's *Lady in the Garden (Saint-Adresse)* (1867), Renoir's *Girl with a Fan* (1881), Gauguin's *Woman Holding a Fruit* (1893), Van Gogh's *Lilac Bush* (1889), along with the Picassos and Matisses, are back where they belong — on view on the walls of the Hermitage.

Paul Gauguin
Woman Holding a Fruit, 1893
The Hermitage has fifteen works by Gauguin, mostly produced while he was living in Tahiti. This painting expresses his ideal of beauty. The woman's face is quiet and immobile. She's reminiscent of a statue carved in wood, but at the same time appears as a majestic and happy human being living at one with nature

Henri Rousseau
In a Tropical Forest: Struggle between Tiger and Bull, 1908
The works of Henri Rousseau occupy a place apart in French art at the end of the nineteenth and beginning of the twentieth centuries. The three paintings in the Hermitage by this ingenious master are excellent examples of his naive art. Rousseau used to like telling stories of his travels to Mexico where he saw "jungles" such as the one depicted here. In real life, the customs officer never left Paris and used to get inspiration from postcards and visits to the zoo

FURTHER READING

To The Hermitage, Malcolm Bradbury (Picador)
Lonely Planet, St Petersburg, Steve Kokker and Nick Selby (Lonely Planet)
St Petersburg, The Rough Guide, Dan Richardson and Rob Humphreys (Rough Guides)
Catherine The Great – a short history, Isabell de Madariaga (Yale University Press)
Catherine The Great – Life and Legend, John T Alexander (Oxford University Press)
Catherine The Great, Henri Troyat (Berkley Books)
Two Comedies by Catherine The Great, Empress of Russia, ed. Lurana Dannels O'Malley (Routledge)
Russia in the Age of Peter the Great, Lindsey Hughes (Yale University Press)
Peter the Great through British Eyes, Anthony Cross (Cambridge University Press)
Valse des Fleurs – A day in St Petersburg in 1868, Sacheverell Sitwell (Faber and Faber)
St Petersburg – A Traveller's Companion, Lawrence Kelly (Constable Robinson)
Images of Space – St Petersburg in the Visual and Verbal Arts, Grigory Kaganov (Stanford University Press)
The Hermitage: The Biography of a Great Museum, Geraldine Norman (Jonathan Cape)
Paintings in the Hermitage, Colin Eisler (Stewart, Tabori & Chang)
Hermitage Magazine, ed. Geraldine Norman (Cultureshock Media)

Graham Addicott is a television producer/director who runs London-based independent company First Freedom Productions, which, along with the Estonian company Allfilm, produced the Five Television series *The Treasures of St Petersburg and the Hermitage*. He and Allfilm's Rein Kotov directed the programmes, which were produced by Pille Rünk.

fivearts

Five
22 Long Acre
London WC2E 9LY

For further copies, please send a cheque or postal order for £5.95 (made payable to Channel Five Broadcasting Ltd) to:
The Treasures of St Petersburg and the Hermitage
PO Box 5000
Manchester
M60 3SU

Or ring the Five order line on 08705 55 50 55
Alternatively, you can visit the Five website at www.five.tv

Also available:
Easter in Art (£5.95), which accompanied the Five Television series of the same name; *Painting the Christmas Story at the National Gallery* (£4.95), which accompanied the Five Television series presented by Dean John Drury; and *Tim Marlow on Tate Modern* (£4.00), which accompanied the Five Television series of the same name

Published in 2003 by Five Television in association with Cultureshock Media to accompany the series *The Treasures of St Petersburg and the Hermitage*

cultureshock

Adam House
7-10 Adam Street
London WC2 N6AA
Tel: 0044(0)207 5209051
Fax: 0044(0)207 5209052

All text © Graham Addicott
Designed by Stephen Coates
Sub editor: Ian Massey
Picture researcher: Juliet Duff
Production manager: Nicola Vanstone
Publisher: Phil Allison

Printed by Friary Press
Repro by DawkinsColour
Distribution by BSS